ART
OF THE
HOUSE

BOBBY McALPINE and SUSAN FERRIER

ART OF THE HOUSE

REFLECTIONS on DESIGN

with SUSAN SULLY

photography by

SUSAN SULLY   ADRIAN FERRIER

RIZZOLI
NEW YORK

New York · Paris · London · Milan

To the ever closeness

of our partners

Ray Booth,

Greg Tankersley,

Chris Tippett,

and John Sease

And for all this, nature is never spent;
There lives the dearest freshness deep down things;
And though the last lights off the black West went
Oh, morning, at the brown brink eastward, springs—

—from *GOD'S GRANDEUR*, by GERARD MANLEY HOPKINS

And the overall effect . . . is love, by which I mean a sense of tenderness toward
experience, of being held within an intimacy with the things of the world.

—from *STILL LIFE WITH OYSTERS AND LEMON*, by MARK DOTY

CONTENTS

The objects we surround ourselves with form our private language. When we put these into play with personal memories, mythologies, and points of view, we express a rich and personal world. —SUSAN FERRIER

ART, ALCHEMY, AND DESIGN

WHEN BOBBY McALPINE AND SUSAN FERRIER DISCUSS DESIGN, they rarely mention color schemes or period styles. Instead, they talk about establishing dynamic relationships between the ancient and the modern, the polished and the raw, nature and artifice, darkness and light. By combining these elements in surprising juxtapositions, they create interiors that are endowed not only with beauty, but also meaning and depth. Bobby uses the term "gilt by association" to describe what happens when a commonplace object is paired with something more refined. A bundle of straw seen in a barn might look ordinary, he explains. But in the company of something gilded, its innate beauty is exposed. Intensifying awareness of its neighbor's opulence, straw returns the favor. Both excavate and expose the other's assets. Susan speaks of weaving together the four elements, the five senses, and intangibles like memory and desire to create layered, nuanced spaces that are as inspiring as they are aesthetically pleasing. She likens this to mixing charms and potions. Both designers use the word alchemy when talking about the art of the house.

Alchemy—the medieval quest to transmute base metal into gold—is a provocative word to apply to design, inciting us not just to mix and match, but to juxtapose things in a way that enhances and magnifies their effect. To begin with the materials of fabric and furniture, carpets and drapery, art, antiques, and decorative objects and unite them in such a way that they are no longer simply a collection of things but also a compound of sensation, emotion, memory, and repose—that is the art and alchemy of home. Interiors created in this spirit are far more than comfortable and pleasant places to dwell—they are spaces that invite those who inhabit them to live deeply, creatively, and authentically. One of the earliest alchemical texts, written in Persia in the twelfth century, is called *The Alchemy of Joy*. That, at root, is what Bobby and Susan practice.

In the company of rough-sawn wood floors and walls, fine gold- and silver-leafed objects appear both precious and elemental. The texture and pattern of a raw pine column glazed with a sheer veil of gray pigment that accentuates its grain is no less beautiful than their dappled metallic surfaces.

Last summer, Bobby and Susan withdrew to the shores of Lake Martin, Alabama, for several weekend-long retreats. They took sanctuary in Bobby's lake house, one of five dwellings designed by the architect on a promontory surrounded by luminous waters. The two had collaborated on the interiors of these houses—all featured in this book—for a decade. Now they returned to this place of rural isolation not for work, but for recreation. Surrendering to the quiet rhythms of the lake, they renewed their creative vision in a summer pastime that turned out to be a profound exploration of the meaning and purposes of design. Earlier that year, Susan had suggested composing and documenting still life-style arrangements as a way to capture in a single instant the way the partners see, think, and create. By summer's end, the two had created dozens of such still lifes—spontaneously assembling three-dimensional expressions of the principles and convictions that shape their work.

Before each weekend, Susan and Bobby collected the ingredients they required—horns, bones, silver, feathers, pearls, stone, wood—and carried them to their secluded laboratory. Instead of smelting them like medieval alchemists in a crucible over flames, however, they arranged them on tabletops and ottomans and allowed the sun that shone through a cathedral-sized window to provide the transforming fire. Surrendering conventional notions about assigned worth or compatibility, they combined raw goods from the vegetable, mineral, and animal kingdoms with silver and ivory from Susan's jewelry box and antiques collected during shared shopping trips to the Paris flea markets and L'Isle-sur-la-Sorge in Provence. When illuminated by the sun's rays and silhouetted against the dark floors, ceilings, and walls of the house, these unlikely compositions became as incandescent and mysterious as the contents of Dutch still life paintings—and equally rich in lessons about the material and spiritual worlds.

Placing one object next to another is a little like prayer or meditation. When I see things that are beautiful in each other's company, it quiets something inside of me.

—SUSAN FERRIER

PAGE 15: *Nature and artifice combine in this corner of a room where branches of coral made of silver hold a genuine nautilus and a nude male figure is immortalized in stone. Succulents shaped like underwater creatures bring life and movement to this arrangement that sits on top of an antique garden table with a zinc base.* PREVIOUS SPREAD: *Arranged before a map of ancient Rome, souvenirs of travel, including antique German postage scales, selenite and pyrite crystals, a bronze cicada from Japan, a Moroccan fertility bracelet, and a sun-and-moon bracelet from Arabia, create a three-dimensional map of the senses and the world.* LEFT: *The varied textures and colors of virgin cedar, broken driftwood, and antique whitewashed lathe offer a natural history of wood in this hallway.*

The arrangements they assembled were whimsical, irreverent, and striking—a puff of mink balanced on the rim of a silver pitcher, a handmade wood and leather boot posed with ormolu candlesticks, vintage pearls paired with freshly caught silver-scaled fish. These compositions explored the complex beauty of nature and its abilities to surprise us and calm us. They revisited the irresistible urge to pick things up—shells, feathers, rare objects in flea markets and foreign bazaars—and to animate our surroundings with them. They explored the power of light and white to refresh the eye and renew the spirit, and the equal importance of darkness and shadow. Among the still life compositions Susan and Bobby arranged that summer were five that corresponded directly to the houses at the lake. Although they were created after the fact, these arrangements might easily have served as maquettes that guided their decoration.

Architecturally, the five lake houses share a strain of DNA. Each employs similar materials, and all of their floor plans feature a voluminous central room overlooking the lake. Within this uniformity, however, the interiors of each reveal surprising individuality. One is a dusky shadow box with burnished highlights of gilt and antique wood. Another is a freshly modern space with uncluttered rooms and broad swathes of white. Combining the textures of wood and stone with serene tones of water and sky, the rooms of one house pay direct homage to nature's beauty. In the dwelling next door, nature and artifice combine to create a setting that is simultaneously primal and elegant. Drawing from a trove of antiques collected in Europe, Susan and Bobby furnished the most primitively designed of the dwellings with some of their rarest finds.

In the following pages, these five houses are coupled with corresponding still life compositions, combining art and design in a way that may, at first glance, seem surprising. Startling us into attention, these juxtapositions open our eyes and hearts to new ways of looking and responding to what we see. Like the alchemists before them, Susan and Bobby know how to mix unlikely ingredients in order to achieve a higher purpose. A list of materials commonly used in medieval experiments would sound familiar to them: metals, pigments, stone, wood, and a compound made by burning bones and horns called 'spirit of hartshorn.' Better known as sal volatile, hartshorn was a popular component of smelling salts—that potent concoction designed to awaken those who had succumbed to unconsciousness. Exploring inspiration and design from a perspective that is equally poetic and practicable, this book has the same intent—to reawaken us to the vivid, unpredictable, and ever-ready beauty that surrounds us, both in and beyond the walls of home.

—SUSAN SULLY

THERE IS LIGHT ONLY IN THE PRESENCE OF DARKNESS. The Italian word *chiaroscuro*—literally "light-dark"—suggests how much one depends on the other. Without the brilliant objects in its center, the dark gray haze in this still life would be nothing but a shadowy void. Animated by their company, however, that murky haze becomes a sensuous bath of black-to-silver shadow. Six objects—a decanter of water, a silver knife and bowl, a peeled orange, and three antique silver bracelets—respond to light in their own ways. The glass decanter, half-filled with water, receives and holds its luster. The silver underside of an upturned bowl shoots it back with a flash. The contours and textures of the silver bracelets reflect the light, casting a mysterious gleam. Although it is the least reflective object in this pile of shiny, polished things, the orange is the brightest of them all. Pulsing with life, its color is vibrant. Peeled and exposed, it is also vulnerable. Light has a heyday with it, crawling all over its skin and illuminating its flesh as if from within. Making everyday objects extraordinary, light has the power to transform them briefly into gold and jewels before the sun journeys on. Held in darkness but caressed by light, the ordinary and the exotic, the perishable and the imperishable acquire equal importance and beauty. The Dutch still life painters knew this when they combined fruit, fish, and freshly killed game with jeweled knives and hand-blown goblets in their compositions. Signaling to one another across the shadows, these objects symbolize life and death, pleasure and suffering, and the transience of time. But they are also simply objects, basking in light. Pointing out treasures one by one through the passing hours, light teaches us that we hold the world in our hands—and shadow reminds us not to forget this nor to take beauty in any shape for granted.

LESSONS
IN
LIGHT

My house at Lake Martin is a carefully calibrated machine for seeing—as well as being—at the lake. Like a camera obscura, it is a plain brown box on the outside with an interior that frames beauty and captures light. In the beginning, the house was what you might expect to find at a lake, with walls and ceilings of wood that blended into the bark of the surrounding trees. But then I decided to conceal the natural grain of the wood—painting the floors and ceilings in shadow and the walls in foggy white. Curtains of charcoal-colored mohair in the central living space added even deeper tones. Mute and monochromatic, the rooms became a kind of laboratory, with light as their primary focus, and the people inside, observers exploring its habits.

The towering living room in the middle of the house is the heart of the laboratory—the chamber where the most exciting discoveries are made. Above, an Empire chandelier with a painted crown and carved tassels offers artificial illumination, but the true source of light is the wall of windows overlooking an infinite expanse of lake and sky. Upon entering the house, this view welcomes you and seems to follow your footsteps from room to room. Already luminous and compelling, the landscape became even more so once it was framed by the dark floor, ceiling, and drapery. This lesson in light is a familiar one. When you hear a noise in the yard at night and wonder what it is, you shut off the lights to better see outside.

A fundamental purpose of this house is to witness what lies beyond it. When a room is in shadow, the shell disappears, allowing the contents to shine more brightly. Silenced, the dark planes of wood and fabric in the house recede like shadows. The subtle colors and textures and simply upholstered furniture also become less dominant, providing a quiet backdrop for the more reflective or textured things around them. Traveling briskly across their surfaces, the light falls on whatever will receive it and pauses, exploding in celebration. Grazed by light, the hand-hewn seat of a cobbler's bench—worn to a satin finish by centuries of use—acquires an unforeseen beauty. Backlit by the giant window, an ungainly chair with hooves and horns becomes a graceful piece of sculpture. It is exciting to observe how indiscriminant the light is, finding and gilding the least-suspected objects in the house. Like Rumpelstiltskin, it has the power to spin straw into gold.

Like the lens of a giant camera, the window in the living room points not only outward, but also inward, collecting light and concentrating it inside the room. Mohair curtains, a Tibetan wool rug, and velvet and linen upholstery in dark shades of gray heighten attention to the reflective qualities and textures of objects made of silver, fur, leather, horn, and wood.

Light's journey through the house offered an irresistible invitation to bring more and more objects into its path, coupling unlikely partners and challenging their compatibilities. Picking up your possessions like plants and moving them into the light allows you to see them all over again. The opulent gilded table inside the front door has no business being in a rural lakeside house, but crowned by a loose bed of stones instead of a slab of marble, its seriousness is leavened by wit. Although its gold legs issue a blatant invitation to the sun's rays, the light is equally content to explore the polished basalt pebbles heaped on top. More gold-leafed objects shine in the house's shadows—a Baroque mirror on a plain wall of painted boards and an empty picture frame propped on a table with tree-stump legs. But light pays no more attention to these bright objects than to the concrete garden statue of a dog that sits on the black floor. Lavishing itself equally on the costly and the commonplace, it shows no sense of judgment or preconception about the value of things. In witnessing this, I am reminded how much beauty lies hidden in plain sight and am made better by this knowledge. A good house will teach you a lesson.

OPPOSITE: *Protected by the overhang of a sheltering roof, a continuous band of windows brings diffuse daylight into the upper reaches of the house. At night, the roof seems to float above the line of glowing windows.* RIGHT: *Like a tree house in the woods, the porch is a place to observe without being observed.*

Riches are always present
as long as we are willing to
make the necessary investment
in time and attention to see
them. The definition of luxury
is to be totally aware of
our surroundings.

—BOBBY McALPINE

ABOVE: *As the hours pass, the living room seems to change its mineral state—alchemizing from sterling silver to gold.* OPPOSITE: *With a curtain wall of glass and screening devices that rarely touch the periphery, the house is secretly modern. You barely notice this because of the aesthetic in which it's dressed. Touched by the light, an antler-backed antique chair from Belgium and plaster-of-Paris bust of a bear in the lounge beyond both appear intensely animated.*

ABOVE AND OPPOSITE: *Surrounded by rustic-modern details, including barn-style doors and a staircase with open risers, a fine antique table from France elevates its surroundings and, in turn, is enhanced through contrast. Like a black frame with a white mat, the surrounding architecture provides a graphic backdrop, accentuating the table's gilded opulence and the surprise of the black basalt stones that fill its bin, replacing the original marble top.*

ABOVE: *A homemade table made from a weathered slab of wood with legs of stumps welcomes the exaggerated formality of an antique picture frame and ormolu candlesticks.* OPPOSITE: *As the longest line that can be drawn through the house, the lateral hallway creates a palatial moment within the confines of its simple container. A power-pole column, a pair of stools upholstered with hair-on-hide, a French Baroque mirror, and a concrete garden statue are among the unlikely company that lines its black-and-white length.*

Seemingly incompatible things, when put together, complement and correct each other. Like marbles in a bag, they polish one another.

—BOBBY McALPINE

ABOVE AND OPPOSITE: *Placed around a teak table with a pale finish, chairs in a variety of styles and upholstery invite you to choose your seat in the dining room. A quilted wall becomes a host for all the exchange that takes place there— silently absorbing the clamor and activity. When you put something so large into so small a space, the effect is quieting. Within this muted setting, a Romanesque baptismal font, cast-iron lion's paws used as candelabras, and a forged-iron pendant attract light.*

ABOVE: *Barn-style doors open to the unexpected opulence of the interior, where gilt and mohair share space with primitive objects and homemade things.* OPPOSITE: *Painting the smallest room in the house dark exaggerates its compression. In its intimate embrace, unlikely elements including a simple three-legged milking stool and fine bronze table find their compatibilties.*

Everything responds differently to light. Mohair and velvet absorb some of its radiance. Well-worn or textured surfaces captivate it, inviting it to pause. Old gold grows more burnished, and polished black floors become glossy and reflective.

LEFT: *A plaster-of-Paris model of a bear's head mounted on a sculptor's stand is a surprising presence in the corner of the kitchen lounge. In this tree house of a room, an antique klismos chair combines the luxury of silver leaf with the simplicity of a caned bottom.* ABOVE: *All the assembled objects—silver hotel trays, plain glass decanters, metal calipers, and compasses—are designed for utility, but they also happen to be beautiful.*

ABOVE: *Bathed in light and shadow, the patinas of tarnished silver and polished concrete are equally beautiful and mysterious.* OPPOSITE: *An elaborately forged piece of iron hanging above the kitchen's concrete island serves no purpose but to lend elegance. Although the kitchen's ceiling is only eight feet tall, casement windows that open like Dutch doors to the surrounding landscape give the room a feeling of expansiveness.*

OPPOSITE AND ABOVE: *Combining a crown of gold-painted metal, which is a poor man's ormolu, with wooden beads that also appear from a distance to be gilded, an Empire chandelier possesses homemade glamour.* PAGE 49: *One of the traits of a dormer window is its ability to intensify the light. This luminous effect magnifies the humble beauty of a nineteenth-century French chair with a white terry cloth seat.*

You may not really notice familiar things that have not been touched for a while until you handle them again or move them about the room.

—BOBBY McALPINE

ABOVE: *Porches generously engage the world. Because it looks as though it were made by enclosing a porch corner, this bathroom has the same relaxed, expansive quality.* OPPOSITE: *Like the old-fashioned sleeping porches they resemble, the guest bedrooms are furnished with simple furniture and white chenille bedspreads.*

Looking in and
looking out—
these may seem
like opposites,
but practiced
together, the
combination
is magical.

—SUSAN FERRIER

The porch, like the house, is covered by the deep overhang of a roof that keeps out the rain and allows those inside to witness their surroundings from a place of shadow.

SURROUNDED BY HORNS, FUR, FEATHERS, STONE, AND SHELL, a pair of shiny white milk pitchers immediately attracts the eye in this still life composition. Strangely enough, their innocent, milky whiteness is the only thing strong enough to cut through all the primal textures surrounding them. In such company, they seem whiter than white, and in comparison to their smoothness, the nearby objects appear all the more rough, ridged, and etched by shadow. White frequently exists in stark contrast to its surroundings—a beacon of reflected light in the midst of a more complicated landscape of color and pattern. By creating neutral zones between competing hues and textures, white subdues their influence. When touched by light, white almost disappears, creating room to breathe and a space to pause and be refreshed. In a composition where all the other objects are so intense and highly wrought, the presence of these large, nearly featureless shapes is essential. They stand apart, but also communicate with their neighbors. White has an ability to draw attention to the reflected points of light that shine around it. Once the eye perceives white, it begins hunting for highlights elsewhere, finding a rhythmic sense of unity. White energizes its surroundings as much as it calms them, revealing a dynamic interplay of light and shadow, color and no color, texture and its absence. Like salt, it brightens the flavor of each individual ingredient. Next to white, everything else finds its truest expression—black becomes blacker and silver shines more brightly. In its absence, colors and textures tend to collide or clamor for attention. Like the dogwood that blooms in the woods in springtime, white endows everything around it with the promise of a fresh start and a new day.

WHEN WHITE IS PRESENT

An escape from the complexities of the urban world, this house is intentionally primal, with cedar walls that are bare of paint or finish. Sanded but unvarnished, they retain the color of freshly milled wood, showing their dark knots and imperfections without self-consciousness. Nature at its most pure, the open-celled wood is naked and innocent. But the intensity of its exposed grain and uninterrupted hue, unbalanced by a corrective gesture, had the potential to overwhelm the generous, open spaces of the house. In order to establish a calm, more nuanced atmosphere, this raw color and texture had to be balanced and their influences reined in. Although we could easily have muted the natural appearance of the wood with paint or stain, we decided to honor it instead, accepting its honey-colored glow as the baseline for every other step.

Wood is a powerful presence, but white is even stronger, offering the only antidote to all the organic texture and tone in the house. If you have something important to say and you want it to be heard, sometimes the best thing to do is whisper. Receding and projecting simultaneously, white whispers this same way. Before white was introduced, the floors and ceilings were stained almost black. Only then was white's energy tapped with cascades of translucent drapery that create an alternate architecture throughout the core of the house. Falling like shafts of light, the seventeen-foot lengths of linen form luminous columns and walls in the central living areas. An exaggeratedly long sofa anchors the room, shimmering like a sail in its center. Slipcovered in white linen, smaller chairs float in the surrounding areas like little islands of light. Upholstered in smooth fabric, these pieces assume a bodiless brilliance in the brightly sunlit rooms.

Once these broad strokes of light and shadow were painted in, the next correction came in the form of smaller, more textured incidences of white. In the living room, two antique lead garden urns with flecked patina are juxtaposed against the sheer columns of drapery. Silhouetted by the room's huge window, a collection of sun-bleached animal horns, which stands on a tabletop of weathered woods, provides a natural history of white. Another expression of white is suggested by the pair of driftwood frames with rough and broken

One of the first things you see when you enter the house is an old leather-bound family Bible on an antique stand. Positioning an object that is so dark and rich in texture and memory against something as fresh as white linen honors it and underscores its importance. This pairing educates the eye, preparing it to better appreciate the other juxtapositions that animate and balance the rooms of the house.

ABOVE: *Although dressed in the same uniform of dark brown wood and a cap-like roof, the houses at the lake each have an entirely different character inside. Like five fiddles playing five different tunes, their shape remains the same, but the song varies.* OPPOSITE AND NEXT PAGE: *Dark floors and ceilings accentuate the warm, natural color of the cedar and its pattern of grain and knots, while also tempering their intensity. In contrast to the newly milled wood, the splintered surface of frames made from pressed driftwood are thrown into high relief.*

surfaces that hangs in the central hallway. These, the most deeply textured objects in the rooms, surround the most polished—smooth glass mirrors that reflect the window's light. This constant rhythm breathes life into the wooden box of a house, adding depth and awareness of the passage of time and its effects.

Color also plays a role in modulating the voice of the unfinished cedar. Directly across from orange on the color wheel, blue cools the temperature of the house. The midnight-blue stripes of a carpet that stretches from the living room to the adjoining study subdue the warmth of the walls. Incidences of metal—wood's opposite in the language of the elements—also establish variation. Metal's presence, from the mottled patina of an industrial table to the dull steel legs of the living room's furniture, presents an alternative to wood's soft density. Suspended in the center of the house like a counterweight, a giant iron lantern balances its energy. In the midst of this dynamic interchange, white always returns. A palate cleanser like sorbet, it is an in-between course that sharpens the senses and provides a welcome pause. White—that pure absence of color—has yet to be muddled by the world. It is the unstained origin to which we must return in order to be refreshed. Lying at the heart of this retreat's serenity, it cuts through all complication and renews the spirit each time you encounter its shining innocence.

The words "white" and "light" can easily be substituted. You can say white and shadow or light and shadow and express the same idea, because white is pure, reflected light.

—SUSAN FERRIER

This is not just a story about white. Another element at play is the use of gigantic scale. Rooms in traditional interiors are often filled with small, leggy pieces of furniture. This house doesn't have any clutter, only large, simple gestures like the huge iron lantern, a long table made of slab wood mounted on steel legs, and tall columns and panels of sheer white linen. The courage of using great amounts of white adds to the apparent volume of the house. When white is present to this degree, you become even more aware of the power of scale.

ABOVE: *Playing games with scale, low pieces of furniture like this primitive antique chair from France, make their surroundings seem all the more monumental.* OPPOSITE: *Within the house's clean, contemporary aesthetic, organic elements like horns and petrified wood reconnect the interior with its natural setting. Surrounded by more linear architecture and furnishings, their natural shapes and textures animate the rooms.*

Painted in with the fewest, broadest strokes, white creates a sense of calm and balance.

—SUSAN FERRIER

The architectural use of the drapery creates a body of white within the wooden framework of the house, softening hard edges and tempering the wood's glow. Large gestures of white arranged symmetrically around the living room quiet the space and unify its mixture of color, texture, and form. Viewed from the second-floor mezzanine, the balance struck by bright shafts of white and accompanying incidences of blue is evident. Because shadows shift in color from black to blue and gray, these same shades were introduced wherever contrast was required. Introducing the element of metal on a monumental scale, the barrel-shaped iron lantern further balances the space.

LEFT: *On either side of the living room, pedestals constructed from whitewashed wood support a pair of equally weathered antique French garden urns. In the adjacent study, lamps made from Victorian architectural fragments stand on a metal table composed of salvaged industrial material. A long rug stretches from the living room to the study, visually connecting the two spaces with its pattern of blue and gray stripes.* ABOVE: *The elements of metal, wood, and horn converge compatibly in this quiet corner of the house.*

ABOVE: *Arranged on the leather console, an antique stone Buddha's head and a string of African currency shells demonstrate the natural spectrum of white.*
OPPOSITE: *In this room where wood, metal, and stone are the only sources of color, every opportunity was taken to introduce a wide range of textures. Within this neutral setting, the tactile differences between a polished slab of pine, soft linen slipcovers, a leather console, millstones, and wrought-iron lamps are magnified.*

LEFT: *Within the geometric lines of the kitchen, framed botanical specimens offer more organic, natural shapes.* OPPOSITE: *A pair of white banquettes receives the bright, reflected light that shines through the kitchen's windows. The cabinets' dark wood, combined with the intermediate tone of polished concrete counters, balance bright white with cooling shadows.*

The material world is filled with infinite natural variations of white—sun-bleached horns and bones, the translucence of quartz crystal formed beneath the earth, and the faded patina of paint long exposed to the elements.

The low walls and sloping wood ceiling of the attic bedroom recall the bare-boned architecture of a camp-style dormitory. Light and shadow move steadily across their planes and angles, creating new shapes and volumes throughout the day. Simple white beds offer a quiet but powerful example of how white creates a place for the eye to rest.

White transports us to an innocent age. As pure and wholesome as milk, it triggers memories of simpler days and invites us to be calm.

—BOBBY McALPINE

With its giant window and overhanging roof, the house is meant to capture and hold the light like a jar filled with fireflies. Although it stands on a tall promontory above the lake, the facade is self-effacing, retiring beneath the shadow of its roof into the surrounding landscape.

EVERYTHING IN THIS STILL LIFE MIGHT HAVE BEEN DISCOVERED ON A WALK by a lake or in the woods—a pair of feathers dropped by a bird, a chunk of mica, waterworn glass floats that drifted ashore, a piece of metal left out in the rain, books carried into the shade for an hour of reading and forgotten there. Although some of these objects are man-made, they all trace their origins in one way or another back to nature. Earth, water, air, and fire—all the elements are represented. Like a pocketful of things picked up and carried home to be looked at and touched later, these mementos evoke a sense of place. Carefully chosen and assembled, they form not just a still life, but also a landscape in miniature. In the way that a painted landscape concentrates the essence of a specific place and time, this composition conveys a stolen moment spent in the heart of the woods, recalling its solace and joy. When natural colors, textures, shapes, and patterns are employed in the design of an interior, they evoke a sense of calm and centeredness just as potently. Materials like weathered wood and roughly hewn stone speak honestly of the ways in which they were formed and how exposure to elements and the passage of time has altered them. In their presence, we are asked to be equally frank, relinquishing manufactured identities and relaxing into a less-contrived self-expression. Reflections of nature transmitted through color and pattern also invite serenity. It's hard not to feel content beneath the blue dome of the sky or a dappled canopy of leaves. When nature and design combine in seamless unity, dissolving the division between what is outside and inside, the invisible walls separating us from our higher selves come down as well. No matter how far we have traveled and how much knowledge and possessions we have acquired, when surrounded by the elements, we are grounded and feel at home.

FROM THE
FOREST
FLOOR

—

Standing solid and symmetrical at the end of a long, straight drive, this house poses as the journey's end. Its wide facade and broad-hipped roof conceal the fact that it is poised on the tip of a magnificent promontory lapped by lake water on three sides. The true drama of the landscape is held back—postponed until you pass through the house's tall front doors and down a narrow vestibule. Only upon entering the room beyond, with its walls of wood and fieldstone and a bay of glass that frames the lake, are you finally delivered to the surrounding landscape. The enclosing walls melt away and you discover that you have not just walked into a house, but arrived at a place where the land meets the water and the water meets the sky. Nothing separates this house from its surroundings. Both exterior and interior are synonymous with the landscape. Like a chameleon that assumes the color of its environment, the house is at one with its setting.

Crossing through the wall of windows, a panoramic vista of the encompassing shore comes inside and spreads its beauty over everything it finds. Like diffused reflections on the still surface of the lake, the contents of the room mirror those of the landscape. Without pretense or exaggeration, they are inspired by it. The subtle pattern of a rug woven in washed-out tones of blue and brown resembles the mottled shallows at the edges of the lake. Wood walls brushed lightly with a greenish-gray glaze appear to have grown a skin of lichen. Textiles evoke the subtlest and often unnoticed nuances of nature—the brown velvet underside of magnolia leaves and the blurred pattern of leaves reflected on water. Linen curtains and upholstery the colors of moss and mushrooms suggest the undergrowth of the forest's floor.

A massive wall of local fieldstone divides the living and dining rooms. Stacked without visible mortar, it appears to have risen directly from the earth. Excavated from nearby fields, the stone literally grounds the house to the land on which it stands. Many species of wood are used in furniture that is not united by any particular period or style. Pine, oak, and walnut mix without contrivance, as they do in the forest. Like the fretwork of branches, the silhouettes of their turned and stick-style limbs create a spontaneous rhythm. You almost find yourself looking for leaves that have fallen to the floor.

Overlooking the woodland shore, the living room's huge bay of windows dissolves the division between the interior and the surrounding landscape. Tall floor lamps made of clear glass are completely transparent and the soft, natural browns, blues, and greens of velvet, linen, and silk are identical to those of the trees, lake, and sky.

ABOVE: *Exaggeratedly tall doors invite you to come inside the house and discover the lakeshore landscape hidden behind its broad facade.* OPPOSITE: *Like the muted colors of the lake in morning mist, the pale blue and green hues of the living room's textiles have a softening effect on the natural textures of wood and raw stone. Constructed of local stone with no visible mortar, the fireplace wall separating the living and dining rooms resembles a slice of natural shale or a stone wall built by a farmer. A landscape depicting the shores of Lake Martin by Michael Marlowe is an appropriately atmospheric painting for the room.*

Each room in the house provides a different way of experiencing nature—sitting by a lake, standing on the edge of an overlook, resting in the shadows of the trees. The living room resembles a clearing in the woods where you can recline on a pillow of moss against a wall of stone, observing the larger world from a place of partial shelter. Like a campsite with logs to sit on and a stone fireplace to gather around, it also is a communal space to celebrate nature's gifts in good company. The dining room on the far side of the wall juts out like a narrow ledge on which to stand and be transported by an endless view. Curtained off from the living room by a soft wall of linen, the cozy lounge is as intimate and safe as an animal's woodland den. From this protected space, broad stairs descend to a screened room for open-air living and dining. Here on the porch, the margins between indoors and out become even more blurred. The moment you descend to its cool floor and feel the breeze coming off the water, all formalities are dropped. Stepping down into the landscape, you know that you are at home in nature and happy to be there.

Recognize and reflect on nature in its most honest and elemental state. There is no need to magnify its beauty.

—SUSAN FERRIER

ABOVE AND OPPOSITE: *The vestibule is compressed by a low ceiling that holds you for a moment before delivering you into the full volume of the house. The rustic pine table, hand-blown demijohns in watery green shades, and landscape painting of trees and sky offer hints of what's to come in the rooms beyond.*

Returning home from expeditions, we bring back souvenirs—talismans endowed with nature's power to ground us with the knowledge that wealth comes not from wares, but from what lies around us.

—BOBBY McALPINE

We want to be
released from the
invisible barriers that
separate us from the
natural world, but we
also crave a comfortable
place from which to
do this—a pillow of
moss or a warm rock
behind our backs.

—SUSAN FERRIER

ABOVE: *Glazed with gray paint, the cedar walls become the color of local stone or lichen-covered bark.* OPPOSITE: *Surrounded by the matte textures of wood and unbleached linen, silks bring the reflective surface of the lake inside. None of this is contrived—even the finest fabrics can be true to nature in color and sheen.* PAGE 99: *Separated from the expansive living room by linen drapery, the lounge offers a quiet interlude before opening to the porch on its other side. Enveloped in nature's neutral tones, it is a place to rest and feel protected in the shadows of the trees. Varied shades of wood, from the glazed cedar walls to the finishes of antique English furniture, become part of the room's subtle palette.*

This room is the quiet hour
you ask for every morning of
your life—a place to sit quietly
and be exactly where you are.
There is a quiet comfort that
comes from being in a place
and feeling connected to it.

—BOBBY McALPINE

We yearn to surround ourselves with nature, even when we are inside. Living grasses refreshed by water, horn carved into beads, dried seedpods, and botanicals that have been pressed, catalogued, and framed are evidence of nature preserved.

ABOVE: *In the dining room—a small alcove on the edge of a promontory where the house stands—a stone wall and velvet settee offer a sense of protection.*
OPPOSITE: *Resembling a slab of wood cut from an old-growth tree, an antique jeweler's table from France takes on the appearance of a naturally occurring form in this woodland setting.*

ABOVE AND OPPOSITE: *On the screened living and dining porch, the variations in the concrete floor resemble the pattern of the soft carpet in the living room. Similarly, its range of wood tones, watery shades of blue and green, and stone echo the living room's design, but in more natural textures and materials. Less plush and more organic, the furnishings speak more directly to the experience of living out of doors.*

Nature surrounds you in its most elemental and atmospheric forms.

—SUSAN FERRIER

Natural wood tones softened by sheer glazes of paint create a restful retreat in the master bedroom. Resembling ripples in water, the striped pattern of the rug contributes to the sense of calm. Corrugated cardboard that recalls the texture of bark frames pages from a naturalist's journal illustrated with pressed botanical specimens.

This house has no wanderlust.
It knows where it is and is
satisfied to be there.

—BOBBY McALPINE

A TRUE SCAVENGER HUNT IS LED BY YOUR HEART, NOT YOUR MIND. When your heart thrills to the chase, it seeks that which it recognizes—a reflection of something that is already within. When an object striking this familiar chord is discovered, there is the sense of encountering a kindred spirit. However haphazard a collection of things assembled in this scavenger spirit might appear, its parts are knit together by an unspoken acknowledgment of who we are and what matters to us. There are reasons why the objects in this still life composition have been chosen and combined. Each speaks of places we want to remember or of destinations to which we have not yet been—of travel, experience, and anticipation. Some have value that can no longer be accounted for—a string of African currency shells, a polished orb of quartz, a Berber silver-fitted horn designed to contain some precious substance. Others are born in utility—feathers from the wings of guinea hens and a Chinese calligraphy brush. Together, they bear witness to the breadth of beauty that surrounds us, reminding us that when cherished, things fashioned by necessity and things designed for the pure pleasure of creation have equal value. Within the shadow box of a dark, neutral setting, the strong individual character of each of these pieces is brought to light and allowed expression without distraction. United by their curved forms, natural patterns, and an organic palette of black, brown, and white, the disparate objects coexist with surprising harmony. Personal and precious to those who discovered them, they need no fancy trappings. They are like the motley items that Boo Radley left in the knothole of a tree or that any boy or girl might hide in a secret place to visit again and again. Speaking directly to and from the heart, they are riches arrayed within life's ordinariness.

WHEN THE
HEART
GOES
HUNTING

Entering this house is like opening a locked trunk and discovering an assortment of favorite possessions, all adventurously won. The furnishings that appoint its rooms—some fine, some primitive, some worn, and some slightly odd—form an unlikely menagerie of characters that have banded together. This mismatched collection of objects, found in the Paris flea markets and L'Isle-sur-la-Sorge, does not represent any kind of premeditated grouping or grand decorating plan. Instead, it is comprised of the spoils of scavenger hunts—unusual pieces that arrested our eyes as we shopped the world, guided not by a list but by the desire to fill up the corners of our hearts. Things that are rough around the edges, made of humble materials, a bit awkward, or highly animated have always caught our eyes and demanded to be brought home. These are sojourners that have seen the world and lived to tell the tale—and they deserve to be honored as much or more than the worldliest prizes.

Unlike its contents, the house that holds these treasures is plain and unaware of being looked at. Designed without pretension, its purpose is not to be admired but to provide a foil for the precious cargo that lies within. Like a boy's secret clubhouse in the woods, its bark-brown walls disappear into the surrounding pines. Within, the rhythms of its stacked cedar boards, square mullioned windows, and open stair risers combine in homemade elegance. True to its natural materials and woodland setting, the architecture is expressed entirely in shades of wood. There is no color inside the rooms—only variations of brown and white. Walls and ceilings of lightly varnished cedar, grounded by darker pine floors, create a completely neutral, natural palette. Everything that is not made of wood wears a uniform of white and beige—burlap curtains, canvas slipcovers, and linen upholstery.

Within this box padded by soft wrappings lie the treasures of the hunt. Surrounded by the living room's simpler fare, two French chairs become the focus of attention. The contrast between the refined calligraphy of their backs and the primitive fur and toes of their feet conjure thoughts of some mythological animal—half human, half beast—that might exist nowhere else but here. Hanging high above the room,

Because so many objects with distinctive personalities populate this house, it was important that the backdrop be united and uncomplicated. Clad in clear-varnished Canadian cedar and dark antique pine, the architecture of the interior is primitive and understated. Decorated in varying shades of natural wood and white, it provides a neutral setting within which more finely crafted objects, including a pair of nineteenth-century French chairs, stand out.

an elaborate chandelier with wrought-iron flourishes and crystal florets seems absurdly formal, yet also totally at ease. Like a shipwrecked treasure washed ashore on a deserted island, this worldly object adds unexpected grace to its humbler surroundings. In the adjoining kitchen lounge, a vintage leather office chair scuffed by years of toil shares the table with three slip-covered chairs, whose simple shapes accentuate the surprising voluptuousness of its tufted curves.

Throughout the wood-lined spaces of the house, the presence of square, solid furniture upholstered in white sets up a rhythmic contrast of light and dark. The geometric patterns of brown-and-white plaid blankets, tiled hangings of framed photographs, and the continuous grid of square window mullions reinforce this rhythm. Repeating the same note from room to room, they pulse as reliably as a heartbeat. This restriction of material, limitation of palette, and uniform baptism in white creates an atmosphere of comfort, familiarity, and trust. Giving generously of itself, the pared-down setting becomes a gracious host, heightening appreciation of the eccentric wayfarers it surrounds. There are places in your life you know are glad to see you and the company you bring—and this is one of them. Somewhere in there is the definition of home.

ABOVE: *Chameleon-like, the house mirrors its surroundings with reflective panes of glass and wood in shades of brown that give no hint of the extraordinary treasures inside its walls.* OPPOSITE: *The leather mailbag hanging on a chair just inside the door is a poetic suggestion of travel and return. It tells the story of someone who has come back from a day's journey and put his work down for the night.*

There is a quality about the house that is as *Saturday* as can be. It is the day you made up all by yourself.

—BOBBY McALPINE

When the big voice
of architecture
is quieted, other
voices that don't
always have a
chance to speak
can be more
clearly heard.

—BOBBY McALPINE

*Unique and confident in nature, the antiques
in this house required surroundings that would
unite with them without competing. Cedar
walls, white upholstery, and plaid wool blankets
provide an uncomplicated backdrop.*

ABOVE: *Many of the pieces we found in France, like this medieval-style pair of andirons forged in the shape of dragons, are highly animated.* OPPOSITE: *The contrast between the delicate backs and robustly carved feet of two nineteenth-century French chairs attracted our attention in the markets of L'Isle-sur-la-Sorge. The wide, square mats of framed photographs, light-colored stone fire surround, and white upholstery accentuate the vibrant lines of these unusual antiques.*

Triple-hinged doors open to transform a corner room into something akin to a screened porch or tree house in the woods. Compressed by a low ceiling, the architecture forces you into the outer environment. As intimate as it is expansive, the kitchen lounge invites you to witness your surroundings in the company of friends. A three-legged English cricket table, vintage leather office chair, and French hall chair all share space in this room where the rules seem to have been relaxed.

LEFT: *With rows of large casement windows opening to the surrounding landscape and a plain concrete-topped island, the kitchen resembles a rustic shelter for cooking and dining in the woods. The white leather banquettes provide comfortable seating, but nature's sights and sounds are the kitchen's real luxuries.* PAGE 127: *The architecture of the interior is unembellished and true to its materials: lightly varnished cedar walls, reclaimed pine floors, and a column made from a pine power pole.*

The wood box of the house is so natural that it almost breathes. Its simplicity creates a sense of ease and familiarity that invites you to rest from your travels and set aside your cares.

—BOBBY McALPINE

LEFT: *Upholstery in shades of white unifies the varied shapes of chairs and stools pulled up around the dining room table while also revealing their differences. Baring the back, legs, and metal ratchets of an antique French chair, the linen upholstery accentuates the simple beauty of its craftsmanship.* ABOVE: *Although the table is a reproduction, the grain of its wood appears just as well used and loved as that of the nineteenth-century French chair beside it.*

ABOVE: *Natural light, a comfortable chair, books to read, and pencils with which to draw—all the essentials for quiet reflection are at hand in this small sitting room.* RIGHT: *There is an honesty to the furnishings of this intimate lounge where soft furniture and plaid blankets say, "Relax and take your ease."*

An eighteenth-century iron chandelier with vestiges of gilt seems fine for this setting, but its foliated iron branches are not entirely out of place in the woods. Burnished by decades of use, the original leather of a vintage office chair matches the cedar walls in rooms where pattern comes in only through plain plaid blankets that are as familiar as a favorite pair of penny loafers, or a child's building blocks.

ABOVE: *A small washroom serves the downstairs dining porch with unadorned utility. Only an antique brass mirror with classical proportions and design hints at the more formal and civilized world.* OPPOSITE: *Instead of doors, burlap curtains partially conceal the kitchen pantry. In a house whose intention is to serve, not to impress, there is no need to hide the implements of living.*

OPPOSITE: *The architecture of the house is unassuming in style. Like a tree fort, it is beautiful because it does not expound upon itself.* RIGHT: *Suspended high above the living room, the chandelier is not visible until you climb the stairs to the second-story mezzanine and discover it at eye level. Seeing it so intimately and unexpectedly, you are all the more delighted to have found it there.*

There is nothing juvenile about this attic bedroom. With bunk beds and antique building blocks, it is a children's sanctuary, but also an adult retreat.

—SUSAN FERRIER

ABOVE: *One of a pair found at the Paris flea market, this vintage bamboo tiki chair is quite at home in the corner of a camp-style bedroom.*
RIGHT: *Belted in glass, the bedrooms resemble sleeping porches. With their continuous bands of louvered blinds, they are also reminiscent of a lumber-mill office where a boy might go to spend a Saturday afternoon while his father worked.*

140

PREVIOUS SPREAD AND RIGHT: *The lower porch's knotty pine walls, cement floor, and screen walls blur the boundaries between indoors and outdoors.* ABOVE: *The simple but carefully crafted details of an antique marble-topped table suggest the handiwork of a country carpenter with an eye for beauty. By pure happenstance, these four letters were all that were left of a collection of hand-carved and gilded letters found in England.*

Camouflaged by color and
kneaded with simplicity, this
house casts shadows on
itself to remain unseen in
the woods.

—BOBBY McALPINE

ELEVATED BOTH LITERALLY AND FIGURATIVELY by the elegant vessel that contains them, the soft leaves of Chinese cabbage acquire a previously unrecognized glamour. At first glance, the pairing of objects seems unlikely, but on closer observation, their affinities are revealed. Framed by luxury, the ribs and fluted leaves of the cabbage appear just as graceful as the silver form that holds them. Equally transformed by juxtaposition, the tarnished curves of the silver bowl are animated by their contents. This is the same gesture expressed in different materials—one mineral, one organic; one perishable, one invulnerable to decay. The sheer unlikeliness of the pairing brings the beauty of both into focus. Both objects were mined, but in different ways. While discovering precious metals requires toil beneath the earth, harvesting nature's humbler gifts demands only that we learn to see in different ways. This second kind of mining is not about the casual glance. It is about learning to look carefully, searching for nature's jewels and recognizing them when we find them. To achieve their highest form, precious metals must be smelted, refined, and shaped by artisans, but nature's jewels need only to be removed from their original setting and recast in unexpected ways to reveal their innate beauty. Treasure lies everywhere, if we are willing to mine the world with our eyes and recast what we find imaginatively. Sometimes we don't recognize how magnificent something is until we see it out of context, framed in a new and unexpected way. By giving permission to unconventional combinations, we invite awareness of the beauty that sleeps around us. Breaking the rules a little bit, such compositions unlock the senses, allowing us to perceive a world that is far richer and more unpredictable than we ever guessed.

NATURE MINED

Built on the piney shores of a lake, this house is inhabited by people who have seen the world and chosen to spend time in the woods. In its rooms, exquisitely crafted objects from Europe share space with nature's simplest gifts, which, artfully presented, seem just as rare and finely wrought. The muse for this project was discovered in a Paris flea market, where we found a collection of birds' eggs mounted inside curiosity domes—the glass cloches popular in Victorian England for displaying natural specimens decoratively. Beautiful in nature, the antique eggs inside the domes appeared all the more so for having been extracted from their nests and mounted on intricate spindles of ebony and agate. Everything about them—their colors and textures, artful presentation, and encasement under glass—became a source of inspiration. Magnified on a larger scale, the collection had the potential to inform the design of the entire dwelling, inspiring its equally unexpected juxtapositions of nature and man-made artifice.

When you enter the rooms of this house, you almost feel as though you have stepped into the domes and are surrounded by the mix of common and exotic eggs they contain. The texture of the walls—washed with a sheer glaze of pearly paint that exposes more than conceals its grain—is eggshell expressed in wood. Although the choice of luxurious silks, velvets, and damasks seems extravagant in this woodland setting, their natural hues reflect the palette of the speckled shells. Even the artwork—etchings of trees, hand-colored illustrations of birds, a bird's nest fashioned from gold—refer back to the ornithological specimens. Actual nests composed of twigs and leaves are also present, displayed beneath another set of antique glass cloches. Arranged beside a giant window that overlooks the wooded shore, these rustic specimens seem to communicate directly with the natural world outside instead of the more refined contents of the room.

Treated as a plain box with rough-sawn walls and floors of lightly sanded, dark-stained pine, the architecture also relates closely to the woodland setting. Organic and unembellished, it provides a perfect setup for rooms appointed in unlikely formality with antique crystal and precious metals. A grand, highly mannered

Two Victorian specimen collections mounted inside curiosity domes anchor the design of the house. Placed on a table inside the dining room's windows, fragile antique nests relate directly to the woodland setting. Antique eggs, more intricately presented on beaded spindles, inspired the juxtapositions of natural objects and man-made artifacts found throughout the rooms. Drawn from the colors of their shells, the dining room's palette of muted gray, brown, and blue reflects their natural beauty, while the painted and gilded chandelier echoes their highly crafted setting.

Italian chandelier with octopus arms and gilded pendants hangs in the center of the house. Although it might easily dominate the space, it is suspended low in the dining room, floating as if in conversation with the eggs on the table beneath. More gilt shines from the carvings of a Baroque chair from France, fragments of an antique European altarpiece mounted like the sun's rays on the rough pine walls, and ormolu sconces. Effervescing through the house like bubbles in champagne, this glittering finery never strays far from nature with decorative details that imitate flowers, pomegranates, fiddlehead ferns, and shells.

This dialogue between the man-made and the natural animates all the rooms of the house, but the unified palette of colors inspired by the eggs prevents it from becoming overstimulating. Objects as far removed in purpose, material, and origin as an industrial steel table, fragile nests, and a pair of gilded stools appear to belong in one another's company within the soft bath of blues, grays, and browns. Like the eggs inside their curiosity domes, they are united by an atmosphere that is serene and almost hypnotic. Suggestive of a picnic in the wild appointed by silver and white linen, this collection of natural and man-made beauty invites us to be more aware of treasure in all its forms. Even the most precious objects are welcome in the woods, and nature's humblest offerings, when asked inside, surprise us with their lavish glamour.

ABOVE AND OPPOSITE: *The reflective highlights of gilded furniture and mirrored tabletops brighten the muted blue-gray palette of the living and dining rooms. Although far less refined, the lightly glazed surfaces of pine walls and a power-pole column coexist harmoniously with luxurious finishes and fine textiles.*

Worldly goods have found their way to this house in the woods where they rub shoulders with finds from nature.

—SUSAN FERRIER

A single object
can inspire a
room, creating
uncontrived unity.
The repetition of
natural elements
throughout the
rooms creates a
visual mantra that
produces a single,
calming tone.

—SUSAN FERRIER

OPPOSITE AND ABOVE: *The industrial material and sturdy construction of a metal table set within the dining room's bay of windows accentuates the fragility of the organic nests that stand on top. Although the table is machine-made, the tree-like lamps on either end look as though they, as well as the nests, might have been brought in from the woods outside the window.*

If you keep up the search with open eyes, you will find that Nature filled a travel trunk with treasures when she created this world.

—SUSAN FERRIER

ABOVE: *Viewed from the small adjacent lounge, the dining room's muted, natural tones provide a quiet backdrop for its surprising juxtapositions of an industrial-style metal table, a gilded Italian chandelier, and natural collections.* OPPOSITE: *Power-pole columns finished with a blue-gray glaze flank the gallery that runs through the house, resembling a pair of trees that have lost their bark. Their natural grain, enhanced by glazing, throws the surrounding gilt and silver into bright relief.*

LEFT: *Rough-sawn pine walls accentuate the refined finish of an antique ormulu sconce from France.* OPPOSITE: *Although they are finished with gold- and silver-leaf, the carved wood of an Italian mirror and nineteenth-century French chair are inspired by natural forms.*

There are grand gestures in the dining room—
the gilded rays on the wall, the opulent chandelier, the triple-tiered window—but there is also
a great deal of imposed intimacy. The curiosity domes draw you in for a closer look and the
compression of the small lounge offers a more
enclosed space from which to witness the drama of the larger room.

OPPOSITE: *The natural appearance of the house's wood surfaces are in character with its rustic, lakeside setting.* RIGHT: *Although the Italian chandelier is elegant in shape and artisanship, its fine finish has been dimmed by time. Upon close inspection, its faded gilt and paint appear more nearly related in tone and texture to the eggs than might be imagined.*

Reinforcing the colors of the eggs through different textures and materials, quartz crystals with blue mineral deposits and hand-dyed silk add depth and richness to the design of the rooms. Crystal, mirrored surfaces, and metal introduce reflected highlights into the muted palette of the rooms.

The home is
the stage from
which we live our
lives—it should
inspire us and
remind us of the
true reasons we
are here.

—SUSAN FERRIER

An antique scale designed to hold metal weights on one side and fruit or vegetables on the other is a subtle metaphor for the aesthetic equation in this house, where objects taken straight from nature are valued as highly as gold and silver. A foxed mirror with a distressed gilt frame brings the reflectivity and finery found elsewhere in the house into the otherwise simple kitchen.

ABOVE: *Although they are impervious to decay, stone figs arranged in an ornate bowl with faded silver plate are suggestive of nature's transient beauty.* OPPO-SITE: *Farthest removed from the house's lakeside view, the television lounge is the only space where nature is held almost entirely at bay. A metal table made from fragments of an industrial container and a sleek steel klismos chair owe nothing to organic form or material. But the fiddlehead-shaped sconce and plant-like pattern of the damask curtains bring indirect quotations of the natural world into this metal-toned room.*

When a house is inspired by a single source, each room becomes a variation upon a theme. In the office, the ivory tones of the eggs are present in leather, linen, wood, and hide. Blue, a strong presence elsewhere in the house, is only hinted at in the cloud-strewn skies depicted in a series of European landscape watercolors. The stylized pomegranates, leaves, and tendrils of ormolu sconces contrast with the graphic horizontal and vertical lines of the office's walls, ceiling, and drapery.

ABOVE: *The master bedroom's monotone palette of gray and white accentuates the varied textures of the furnishings. Antique crystals look like drops of dew against a backdrop of moss-soft velvet and satin pillows that resemble the smooth caps of mushrooms growing in the bracken of the forest's floor.* OPPOSITE: *The columns of gray velvet framing the bed mirror the forms of an ancient temple depicted in the antique print hanging on the rough pine wall.*

In the master bedroom, a limited palette of grays, from light to dark, conveys a sense of calm. Enclosed by the bedroom's rough board walls and ceilings, a bed draped in heavy velvet creates a sumptuous room within a room. Inside its velvet walls, silk satin pillows, crystal lamps, a hair-on-hide table, and unbleached linen combine in a kind of primal elegance. Positioned near a bay window surrounded by trees, the bed is an opulently appointed nest in the woods.

ABOVE AND RIGHT: *An arrangement of white peonies and antique silver bracelets on a nearly black surface expresses in small scale the attic's interplay of light, dark, and reflective materials. Silhouetted against dark cypress walls, the light-colored bedding and natural fleece pillows resemble the peony's pale petals. Lamps made from wood dipped in silver are the jewelry in the room, catching the eye and inviting you to look more closely. Shaped like tree trunks, the lamps also make reference to the bird and tree imagery found in the rooms below.*

The contrast between the guest bathroom's nearly white walls and cabinetry and ebony-colored floors and blinds offers a dynamic study in dark and light. The room's rectangular and oval forms and the stripes of its horizontal blinds are highly geometric in form. Only the tree-like floor lamp calls nature back into play.

ABOVE AND OPPOSITE: *The enclosed porch on the lower level of the house is physically one step closer to nature than the more formal living and dining rooms above. Simply decorated with more organic furnishings, including rattan furniture, linen slipcovers, and a stone garden urn, the sitting area has no gilt or silk details; its only metallic highlight comes from a shiny chrome lamp.*

LEFT: *An antique table made from a thick slab of wood could easily be imagined as a giant's picnic table in the woods. Its natural, organic surface crowned with a silver urn recalls the mix of nature and man-made finery in the more formal room above.* ABOVE: *Hung just inside the front door, an artwork featuring eggs and a nest displayed in a frame within a frame is a perfect visual metaphor for the theme of nature removed from context and reframed.*

PERSONAL PERSPECTIVES

Susan, love, it's late. I am lakeside. Though I bedded down early, I'm up and on the side porch as if I were whispered to again to sit up and take notice of a good day passed and another coming. Here in the wee hours, I feel like a thief, this "time" stolen from an account I didn't know I had. Not long from now, I know I'll witness a sight to be seen, if I just tune myself to notice. Yesterday at dawn, as I wandered down the stairs, I was struck to find I was not the first to enter. Light had slid in sideways to touch and caress only certain objects. Realms of darkness remained. I was hushed by the contrast. I silenced my movement so as not to disturb or stop it from happening. It was enough to watch the rays unfold over the morning hours.

This cabin, one of several, was designed to witness the lake from the wooded hills. Hence, it is a simple box, dark in value so as not to make noise. The irony is that in letting nature rule, the cabin and its contents are enhanced. It is by accident that I have built a camera obscura, and I live in it, and lessons uninvited pour over me. Here, firewood and gold are almost indistinguishable from each other. It is as if everything is elated and has become gilded by their association. Won't you come and help me see how to put to work these lessons in light? Bring your tall friend with the good eye, and your little dog, too.

Bobby

Dear Bobby,

We are on our way, and with me come adored treasures gathered during my travels. It would be wonderful to survey them with fresh eyes. Berber silver, Icelandic furs, stolen feathers, strings of amber and pearls, stones, bones, orbs of color, and savage jewels—anything that communicates or informs a feeling or mood is what compels me. Like talismans, they recall extraordinary moments and memories—a reminder to me that there are many ways to see and experience what lies around us. Bringing mementos from around the world into a domestic setting gives them new life and redoubles their meaning. I look forward to seeing how their importance and beauty can be magnified through our collective vision. I sense that something important is about happen.

Love, Susan

Dear Bobby,

In play is where invention lives. To talk about work in terms of labor is to lose that sense of play and spontaneity. To work with someone with the same purpose is a privilege. What we have created from the pieces that have been brought together is akin to conjuring a spirit—our phoenix. How we view this time together at the lake has filled me with wonder. We trust in our collaboration to obtain beauty in everything. We continue to learn from each other, and our bond is exhilarating. Let us hope that what has been an extraordinary experience for us will set off a chain reaction inspiring others, and that they, too, will share our desire to surround themselves with "art of the house."

Yours, Susan

Susan, I'm alone just now, here again lakeside. I'm left to ponder our experiment. I'm wondering what tapped us this summer past to roll from our beds and record what we witnessed. And now, printed on these pages, are the fruits of our work together. What was leaned into has become this book. The summations of days, the wide-eyed admissions of fireflies caught before they could flee, moments savored as they were happening have changed me. I am more prone now to stop midstream and claim what's in front of me. My concept of real estate has advanced past studs and stone. I was not alone; I was with you. As our lessons silt down through us, I am forever grateful for this happening. It is good to know that lessons come and go, but also good to know that they come again. Faith of months, faith of years, become us, most beautifully lit in summers to come.

Bobby

ACKNOWLEDGMENTS

A STILL LIFE IS MADE OF DISPARATE THINGS—*each beautiful in its own way and each contributing something different and essential to the composition. That is the source of its power to elevate and transform. The same can be said of this book and those who joined together to compose it. We offer our heartfelt gratitude to all of you: the homeowners Donna and Ted Giles, Donna and Kerry Hand, Betty and Jody Saiia, and Michelle and Austin Singleton; the partners and staff members of McAlpine Booth & Ferrier Interiors and McAlpine Tankersley Architecture; coauthor and principal photographer Susan Sully; still life photographer Adrian Ferrier; graphic designer Eric Mueller; editor Sandy Gilbert Freidus; and publisher Charles Miers.*

Born in an Alabama sawmill town, BOBBY McALPINE designed his first house at the age of five and hasn't stopped since. Although he holds degrees in both architecture and interior design, he continues his lifetime of learning in the world's classroom. Architect, romantic, poet, and entrepreneur, he has gathered an eclectic family of professionals for his firms, McAlpine Booth & Ferrier Interiors and McAlpine Tankersley Architecture, now in its thirtieth year. SUSAN FERRIER, raised in upstate New York, found herself graduating with a fine art degree in interior design in the Deep South. Her varied life experiences have shaped an exceptionally intuitive and perceptive approach to design, which led to a partnership with McAlpine and Ray Booth in 2000. Extensive travels with her husband, native New Zealander Adrian Ferrier, and the collections of jewelry and natural history specimens she has gathered along the way, are among her deepest sources of inspiration.

The two firms work both independently and in collaboration, attracting clients from across North America and beyond. Their designs include hundreds of residences, restaurants, a chapel, follies in a public park, and a family compound on a private island in the Caribbean. Their portfolio has been published in books and periodicals including *Veranda*, *Architectural Digest*, *House Beautiful*, *Southern Accents*, *Elle Decor*, *Southern Living*, *House and Garden* (both American and British), *Garden and Gun*, *Coastal Living*, and *Traditional Home*. Bobby's furniture line, McAlpine Home, is available nationwide. His first book, *The Home Within Us*, is a Rizzoli bestseller.

SUSAN SULLY is the author, coauthor, and photographer of many books about architecture and design, including *The Home Within Us* and her recent solo project, *Houses with Charm: Simple Southern Style*.

Opening to what is around us, we learn to see again.
We also open to ourselves and know that we are home.

—BOBBY McALPINE

PAGES 194–195: *An Elizabethan box holding a collection of cherished letters, a sixteenth-century box filled with a loved one's ashes, communion cups, and a walking cane with a compass in its handle form a still life composition that celebrates love, life's journeys, the ephemeral, and the eternal.* PAGE 197: *Including silver, pearls, a shell, fur, and wood, this still life composition is a study of nature's beauty, both refined and in the raw.* PAGE 198: *African currency shells and an eccentric horn chair from Belgium are souvenirs of foreign expeditions taken with eyes attuned to unexpected beauty.* PAGES 200–201: *Sheer glass beakers and solid silver bracelets melt into pure white light when illuminated by the sun's glancing rays.* RIGHT: *Held open by a handmade carpenter's rule, a volume on the architecture of David Adler sits atop a French Art Deco table made of steel with brass appointments.*

PHOTOGRAPHY CREDITS: All photographs by Susan Sully except, by Adrian Ferrier, pages 4, 10 (right), 16–17, 21, 24, 25, 41 (left), 55, 83, 111, 133 (left), 149, 168, 169, 170 (left), 171 (right), 192, 194–195, 197, 198, 200–201, 205; Eric Mueller, pages 10 (left), 11, 75 (right), 93, 100 (left), 101, 171 (left), 204 (right); and authors' photograph by Erica George Dines, pages 202–203.

First published in the United States of America in 2014 by Rizzoli International Publications, Inc.
300 Park Avenue South, New York, New York 10010
www.rizzoliusa.com

Page 6, Quotes from Gerard Manley Hopkins, *God's Grandeur, Gerard Manley Hopkins: Poems and Prose* (Penguin Classics, 1985); Mark Doty, *Still Life with Oysters and Lemon* (Beacon Press, 2001).

2014 2015 2016 2017 / 10 9 8 7 6 5 4 3 2 1
Printed in China
ISBN 978-0-8478-4253-7
Library of Congress Control Number: 2013953188

Project Editor: Sandra Gilbert | Graphic design by Eric Mueller/Element Group

CASE FRONT: *Burnished by time, gold and silver leaf and the fading mercury glass of an antique mirror exist in harmonious counterpoint with rough-sawn pine walls and the dark polish of ebonized floors—each honoring the other's essential beauty.*